YOUR KNOWLEDGE HAS VALUE

- We will publish your bachelor's and master's thesis, essays and papers

- Your own eBook and book - sold worldwide in all relevant shops

- Earn money with each sale

Upload your text at www.GRIN.com
and publish for free

Bibliographic information published by the German National Library:

The German National Library lists this publication in the National Bibliography;
detailed bibliographic data are available on the Internet at http://dnb.dnb.de .

This book is copyright material and must not be copied, reproduced, transferred, distributed, leased, licensed or publicly performed or used in any way except as specifically permitted in writing by the publishers, as allowed under the terms and conditions under which it was purchased or as strictly permitted by applicable copyright law. Any unauthorized distribution or use of this text may be a direct infringement of the author s and publisher s rights and those responsible may be liable in law accordingly.

Imprint:

Copyright © 2014 GRIN Verlag, Open Publishing GmbH
Print and binding: Books on Demand GmbH, Norderstedt Germany
ISBN: 978-3-668-04802-7

This book at GRIN:

http://www.grin.com/en/e-book/304607/greenpeace-s-unfriend-coal-campaign-and-facebook-a-case-study

Joel Diener

Greenpeace's Unfriend Coal Campaign and Facebook.
A Case Study

GRIN Publishing

GRIN - Your knowledge has value

Since its foundation in 1998, GRIN has specialized in publishing academic texts by students, college teachers and other academics as e-book and printed book. The website www.grin.com is an ideal platform for presenting term papers, final papers, scientific essays, dissertations and specialist books.

Visit us on the internet:

http://www.grin.com/

http://www.facebook.com/grincom

http://www.twitter.com/grin_com

Chair for Christian Social Ethics and
Social Policy
Advanced Business Ethics - SS2014

Case Study Report

Greenpeace's Unfriend Coal Campaign and Facebook

Due date: June 23th, 2014

Table of Contents

Executive summary 1
I. Statement of the problem 2
II. Causes of the problem 2
III. Recommended solution, decision criteria and alternative solutions 3
IV. Implementation and justification 3
V. Conclusion 5
VI. External Sourcing 6

Executive summary

Once Facebook announced its plan to build a facility in Prineville, it was confronted with critics from the society lead by Greenpeace through their official Facebook profile and Youtube video. Greenpeace objected the decision of Facebook to work with an energy supplier (PacifiCorp) who produces the energy mostly from coal. Greenpeace stated that Facebook should set a positive example for the industry and is financial secured to influence the mixture of their energy supply.

So now is the question which strategies are possible for Facebook to realize the plan for the facility which will support the economical weak community without endangering their reputation?

Facebook therefore can either ignore the public campaign of Greenpeace or completely comply to the demands of Greenpeace which comes with huge investments loss. Or they find a solution which enables them to proceed with their original plan of Prineville and to satisfy the public demands of the society and Greenpeace by altering the plan a little bit for data center to make it more sustainable. Facebook can show sincerely their concerns towards the environment and its responsibilities by collaborating with Greenpeace and other high-tech companies to research and develop renewable energy supply solutions for the future. This research will also benefit other companies. The before mentioned involvement strategy will display their Corporate Social responsibility because their promotion takes advantage of their core business respectively their strength. Also Facebook can proof that business ethic can create competitive advantages and isn't at cost of shareholders. They will even boot the firm's growth and development in the long run.

I. Statement of the problem

After announcing its expansion in 2010 Facebook was confronted with critics from Greenpeace. The NGO (non-governmental organization) Greenpeace found fault with the energy supply of the new Data Center of Facebook in Prineville, Oregon. Even though Facebook stated that the new Center would be highly energy efficient, for example, the company intends to reuse the server heat. In addition the favorable climate conditions enable Facebook to reduce operating costs.

However Greenpeace publicizes on Facebook itself that the energy supplier for the facility gains it energy from coal, which is one of the catalyst for climate change. So Facebook is under public pressure to resolve this issue without endangering its ongoing plans for the facility and losing its follower while experiencing reputation damage. What are possible actions for Facebook regarding the campaign of Greenpeace?

II. Causes of the problem

Greenpeace is a non-governmental organization founded in the 1970s which try to make the society aware of issues regarding pollution, nuclear power, oceans, forest and climate change. Its style of operating is in a non-violent way and independent from governments and companies.

On the other hand Facebook is a fast growing social network with over half a million users worldwide after it was established by Harvard students in 2004. In order to provide the needed capacity for handling all customer demands Facebook wanted to build a facility which would meet the technical requirements. Considering all aspects Facebook decided to build the facility in Prineville, Oregon. Prineville offers favorable climate conditions which allow cooling the server heat with cold outside air. Furthermore the local government would subsidy the project and the facility will offer employment to the location which suffers under the crisis, 20% unemployment rate.

While the plans are starting to take shape, Greenpeace suddenly starts a campaign focusing on Facebook against energy generated by coal. Greenpeace complains that Facebook has enough financial power to influence where the energy it used comes from. Moreover as the leading social network it should set a positive example for other companies in the industry. Greenpeace also used its Facebook account and a Youtube video against Facebook itself. Under the public pressure with increasing followers Facebook has to answer to the critics without slowing down the construction process and damaging its image.

III. Recommended solution, decision criteria and alternative solutions

One possible action for Facebook would be to ignore the critics and the pressure from Followers of the unfriend coal campaign, because people tend to forget fast. Furthermore only 0.1 % of Facebook users noticed the campaign of Greenpeace. When Greenpeace has found a new hot topic it will shift its direction to another victim. During this time Facebook should just keep a low profile and wait until the big attention is over.

The second possibility would be to attack Greenpeace directly and wrest the power from Greenpeace to manipulate the public. Facebook should also make public that Greenpeace also used coal energy. Furthermore Facebook is not the only big company that uses energy produced by coal because they have limited options to choose looking at the existing energy mix in the United States. In the USA only 9% of their energy mix consists of renewable energy. Facebook can upset the public about the authenticity of Greenpeace when pointing out Greenpeace's own faults and problems while ensuring the public how energy efficient the new facility will be.

Another strategy would be to discuss the issue calmly with Greenpeace to regain the trust of the customers. Facebook can try to explain once more the advantages of the current plan for the facility and might reach a solution with Greenpeace in a more peaceful way than the former suggestion. Furthermore Facebook can ensure that they will work with Greenpeace and other big companies like Google, etc. to research alternative solutions with renewable energy.

The last alternative would be to comply and change the current energy supplier or even the location which will cause a lot of problems like investment costs and the delay of the current schedule. But with an energy supply from renewable resources Facebook can be pioneer in the social network industry and be a role model for many others. This will surely boost Facebook's reputation and it can gain advantages from it. Also Facebook which now connects over 1.28 billion users (March 2014), has a responsibility to exhibit good corporate citizenship toward the public it serves. It's not enough for a company with such a huge customer base to be only efficient in providing its services. Facebook is acting globally and it has the power to make a positive contribution to the society and the world by choosing the right kind of facility, for instance.

IV. Implementation and justification

Well, the first suggestion is really risky. Ignoring the events can be disadvantageous when the situation gets out of hand and Facebook can't restore its image anymore. Moreover, most of the users of Facebook are young so they pay attention to the environmental impact.

On the other hand, to beat Greenpeace at their own game Facebook has to proceed cleverly and with outmost care when trying disempowering Greenpeace and to reclaim its power over the public opinion. But Facebook shouldn't submit to the pressure of Greenpeace and show society how common its way of operating is. A successful implementation of this solution will avoid costs of altering the current project. Furthermore Facebook can use the letter of Greenpeace with its offer of finding a solution together as a chance. They can invite the public to the discussion and turn the table. All these actions acquire personnel, money and time which are needed to complete the campaign. Furthermore a negative strategy which only blames one another is unlikely successful. Facebook needs to show positive results to regain the trust of customers. So they should not just perform the inform strategy but respond directly to Greenpeace and the Facebook users.

Another issue is that the demands of Greenpeace are unrealistic. Facebook can't change its plan that easily, considering the existing energy mix in the US. Additionally they need to consider the effort, time and investment cost for the Prineville facility. Also they bring hope to the economy because they will create a lot of workplace and other beneficial projects for the commune like funding of local school projects and display corporate citizenship. Therefore changes need to come step by step like suggested before in collaboration of different companies e.g. Google, Apple, etc. in a research center for renewable energy solutions for technical enterprises. Furthermore Greenpeace can't set a deadline 2021 or agenda for another company, Facebook itself needs to commit themselves to environmental friendly goals if they want to achieve them. Moreover it needs to be mentioned that thanks to the decision of Facebook to settle in Prineville, Google also opened a facility there and gives opportunities to the commune. Again, Facebook will reassure the public it will prefer the usage of green energy where it is possible. Furthermore Facebook can offer Greenpeace cooperative work for their campaigns to make the Facebook users more aware of Greenpeace's activities and concerns. Because communication is the core business of Facebook, so they should be able to link their CSR activities to them and show more engagement. So Facebook can 'do good and talk about it' to increase their popularity like in an ideal corporate citizenship.

One more possibility for Facebook to show their sincere efforts to promote green energy would be to issue a CSR (corporate social responsibility) report. A non-financial report would reduce the information asymmetry and as a consequence create trust. Followers are informed about the activities of Facebook and its impact towards environment and society. Facebook will be able not only to demonstrate its business ethics but also its environmental ethics. They can take advantage of a brand strategy and be the industry leader for social networks which operates with renewable energy. There is also a possibility of a branch strategy when they function as a role model to revolutionize the whole industry sector. This will create a competitive advantage on the meso-level for a more sustainable growth because the report enables Facebook to have a holistic view of the management decisions.

Employees of Facebook will have more confidence since they work for a firm with a good reputation. This will reduce absentees and motivate them to show more commitment.

Considering the last proposal it would avoid further confrontation with Greenpeace but will increase the costs for the facility. Maybe in the end the location must be changed and all the planning went for nothing. Then Facebook has to start from the beginning and it will be unclear when a new facility will be build. Not to mention the negative impacts for the community in Prineville. But on the other hand if such a huge company like Facebook outsources due to environmental reasons the USA might consider their current energy mix again. For example the newest data center of Facebook was built in Sweden which is completely operated solely on wind energy.

After considering all aspects the third proposal, the involvement strategy, would be prudent because their consequences are minimal. Moreover they will bring Facebook long-term benefits and guarantee a sustainable growth for all the stakeholders.

V. Conclusion

Given its growth projection, failure to solve the dirty energy issue keeps Facebook and other 21st century innovators locked into 19th century energy choices. Just as high tech companies have revolutionized our lives in so many ways, they need to help transform our production and use of electricity so that modern technologies can be supported by clean, renewable and modern energy choices.

All in all Facebook needs to take action soon otherwise Greenpeace's power over the project will grow even more. It would be wise for Facebook to transform this risk into a chance through brand strategy. Maybe even a branch strategy to change the whole sector by placing an example. By building a research center through collaboration it will benefit Facebook in its decision for energy usage. By following an involvement strategy and engage actively in the discussion for more green energy, Facebook can display a good corporate citizenship. Using its communication channels to promote clean energy, Facebook can link CSR to their core business and make themselves resistant against competitors. Furthermore the disadvantages of information asymmetry can be reduced through a CSR report to gain trust of the society and to have a special trait as a competitive advantage like ethical business and employer. In the long run this will encourage sustainable growth and a broader customer base. Costs like absenteeism and employee fluctuation can also be reduced.

VI. External Sourcing

Greenpeace (2010): Facebook: Unfriend Coal, GreenpeaceVideo, Vancouver, http://www.youtube.com/watch?v=QPty-ZLbJt0 (access: 09.06.2014).

Ligett, B. (2011): Facebook teams up with Greenpeace to kick coal power to the curb, Inhabitat Internet Brands Inc., El Segundo, http://inhabitat.com/facebook-teams-up-with-greenpeace-to-kick-coal-power-to-the-curb/fb-greenpeace-coal-2/ (access: 09.06.2014).

Sayer, P. (2012): Facebook Unfriends Coal – Friends Greenpeace in clan energy campaign, IDG Media Pvt. Ltd, Bangalore, http://www.cio.in/news/facebook-unfriends-coal-friends-greenpeace-clean-energy-campaign-213192012 (access: 09.06.2014).

Van Horn, J. (2011): Greenpace calls upon Facebook to unfriend coal, Guardian Professional Network, London, http://www.theguardian.com/sustainable-business/blog/facebook-unfriend-coal-greenpeace (access: 09.06.2014).

YOUR KNOWLEDGE HAS VALUE

- We will publish your bachelor's and master's thesis, essays and papers

- Your own eBook and book - sold worldwide in all relevant shops

- Earn money with each sale

Upload your text at www.GRIN.com
and publish for free